Mother

Elizabeth Blackwood

BookLeaf
Publishing

India | USA | UK

Presentation by *BookLeaf Publishing*

Web: www.bookleafpub.com

E-mail: info@bookleafpub.com

ISBN: 9789357446396

First edition 2022

DEDICATION

To my beautiful family who made me who I am, to love, to beauty, to healing and to all the blessings we hope for in the future. To my husband who encouraged this and everything that I've ever done that's been worth anything. To God who made everything so delicately and powerfully that we write poetry about it.

Beginning

Birthed in that pressured darkness
An adult
Limbs fully formed but out of control
Head replanted and oriented edgeways
Another name
Another place
It seems almost another time
To be clean, clean, cleaned
Report for duty
There are things to be done.
And things to be undone.
No time to grieve the severing of the entwined
The distance between
The stranger beside
The rope of a shared experience torn asunder by
biology
Report now
The test begins now
It's one you have no hope of winning, but try
anyway
Don't take the moment to love
And be loved
Succeed. Now. Right now.
Or else they will be called.
The ones we do not speak of.

And torn asunder again you shall be.
So hurry
The test begins

The Dandelion Girl

We are trying you and I
We have our Bambi legs
We wobble together and fall together
How beautifully precious
That wonder
The wonder of all things
Lighted anew
Fresh and clean like spring grass
A fingertip touches a fingertip
A joining like the creation of Adam
But no regal nose bridges are needed here
All is softness and light and newness
That touch of someone so small
Our fingerprints align for a moment
And I image the microscopic details of our
atoms aligning
Ridge to ridge
Locking together like tracks
There is the connection still
Something that was once thought to be missing
and severed
But there still, in consciousness and presence

A tender merging of electricity
Warmth and gentleness
And your eyes looking to me
I am fumbling but you are patient
You have waited a whole internal lifetime after
all
A dandelion smile you gift me
And a weary willow one I return

Cloth not Glass

There is a courage that is missing now
A strength in the back and legs
A stillness in the hands
Now I am fidgeting and eyes dart
Afraid, and insecure equally
Where did that strength come from
And more importantly
Where did it go?
Where was the fully formed human being
That skipped up mountains and faced demons
with a wry smile
Is she absent or deceased
Has some long journey with an adventurous side
quest waylaid her
Or has she sunk deeper into that abyss that does
not end
That we do not know of
The wind batters and it is a wind made of voices
Unsolicited by still invited in
For who wants to ignore advice given
If something were to happen
And there you are.
A steadying hand.
You are doing well.
Do not look behind unless with compassion

Do not look ahead except with excitement
And now it seems that strength was brittleness
A shattering sugar glass
So easy to tear into and devour
It is easy to be strong if inflexible
Not so when you must be molded to another
For softness it must be
There is nothing soft in glass
This I know
For too many times have I leant against it
seeking comfort
And found only the cold and sharp
So a new found wisdom
Be formed by weaving not by fire
Be like cloth not like glass

3am

There is an effervescent incandescence at 3am
Unmarred by the third hour of horror viewing to
keep me watchful
The stillness, I wish that I could go back to
Even in the time before
I longed for the night
To walk alone in the city and feel the slumber
Like a collective sigh
And myself the watcher who gets to breathe in
the breathing out
The world itself shifts in with the breath
And out with the breath
It groans and mutters, day creatures stirring
through minor disruptions
Humans safe in their reinforced constructions
Open the door
Let in the breathing
From your lungs to mine
Nevermind the time
Let's come together in the blue
And have silhouettes mesh into nightmare
creatures
Let's use candles and flickering shadows
Instead of neon pulses
And watch the sleeping children
And sigh to ourselves in the contented stillness

Back to Work

How is it three months already?
How is it only three?
Each step taken is a symphony of instinctive
wrongness
Pulsing down the DNA strand
Into each cell and fibre
There is something wrong with this
The number 13 seems important
A beginning and an end
Twisted on its head
Now a 31 instead
Our civilized process and industrial proceedings
Have not accounted for this raw moment
And its needs are unmet
And ignored
Suppress down the instinct
Hold onto the logic
Don't question the rightness of a system of
progress
Because progress gave you what you have
With minimal risk
Not none though.
But the flower blooms through the cracks
Or at least the weeds do

Is it a flower or a weed that strangled the throat
right now
And causes the tears to flow
The turned face, mine or yours
And abandonment
Mine or yours?
Do you sniff after my absence
Or are you gently taken enough
That I am not necessary
And you are comforted
Which do I want?
Do I want that answer?

Thoughts on Pain

We have such violent beginnings
No wonder we expect such violent ends
We crave the moment of test
To prove to others that we are enough
It is splintered along the lines of gender
This moment
Aztec women were warriors
Battling against the Gods for the soul of their
child
And you can see that battle
In the strain and exhaustion
The blood and vomit
The screams
So much like a battle scene
And yet we profess its normalcy and naturalness
It is natural, yes, but normal?
Labour pains for an apple
Or for knowledge and choice
Cursed for generations
The only beginning to man to be violence
Violence begets violence
Every individual created and conceived
Birthed and to breathe
Through violence
Will a machine take away the sin as the pain

There are those who relish the penance
Make me pure, make me whole
Pain is sin passing from the body
Pain is penance
Pain is pressure
But not
Let us not say that pain is pain
For beauty cannot come alongside pain.
And this is where we are wrong
The greatest beauty came from pain
The salvation of sinners
The birth of all
Pain and beauty are brothers
Sisters perhaps moreso
For who has not known the moment of pains
relief and not felt that the world were more
beautiful hereafter?

Tending the Orchard

May we be an orchard
Rich and fertile
For you to plant your roots
Too many raised in concrete jungles
Models of efficiency
Homes to grow strength and posture
But none of inner stillness
Or the other
The calm that hides the storm
Or that neutrality that comes from caring not
Never engage, remain apart
Smile to Stepford and pawn your losses
Is there life in the ecosystem of hidden
mushrooms and cherios strewn
Of stains and discolouration
The growth of a garden expedited by the death
of the other
The decay and the damp
Is it the same for a person?
What fruit would it produce?
And by which name will it be known?
And is the fruit really a reflection of the soil
Or of the tree itself?
For we are not the tree and you the blossom
To think so would be gratuitous

But let us be the orchard
Where you and your other trees and flowers
stand tall
Blooming and giving fruit as desired
And may the soil be rich enough
That you are never drawing from an empty well

The Empty Chairs

The circumstances suggest it will be no
There is impossibility in the desires
That these others will not ever be able to be
And I feel that loss
The empty chair, left empty instead of set aside
The feeling that someone or someones are
missing
And it is my own failing that insists
I cannot be good enough
To earn the blessing
As though blessings can be earnt
As though anyone could earn this
For what would I have to do to earn this
Or do I need simply to ask?
Is there virtue in the asking
More than the getting
A humility that creeps through the cracks
A vine through a wall
Or is a gift merely a gift
How have we perverted the gift in its fairness
Capitalism prescribing the level of gift for
relationship
Buy multiple to be safe
And line the pockets of the prosperous
How do we respond when the Father presents

With fear as gift is responsibility
Or a reflection of our own ineptitude
I hope not
I desire this future
And these missing someones
But gratitude is a balm
A gratitude for the ones already gifted
Can it allay
Or will I always been looking and longing
Towards the empty chairs
That I refuse to put away?

Progressive Opinions

November is dressed in your pale face
And October the dark hair of hers
Secret and unbegotten things
Desires whispered, never spoken
Is it such a dirty thing
To love
And to love openly
Robust and welcoming
It is against the control of things
For those who do not want
They seek a virtue for what they fear is
selfishness
Preservation or control
Keeping all things clean
And as they were before
The irony of progress and conservation aligned
Enlightened tradition
Love on the moors
Where the bodies are hidden
This is a new dialectic
Caring for others is selfish
Living for self is sacrifice

This new enlightenment
Renaissance of hedonism
But whitewashed and rebranded anew
Because progress is virtue and vice

Learning to Speak

Your eyes are watching my lips
As though seeing would process the sound better
Squawks are not enough for you now
You wish to be heard
And more than heard
Understood
These strange syllables and specific sounds
That now, in your deep thought, have meaning
Are they a new toy for you?
The patterns are fascinating
As much as the black and white stripes
And blurs of colour
In your early days
Now the sounds are a cacophony of meaning
And this learning will never cease
Does it make you feel exhausted?
Soon it will be not just the sounds
But the tone
The minor inflection of pitch and dynamic
As delicate and incomprehensible as a
symphony
To the unspecialized
So much meaning
But will it be translated
Or will we be forever in isolation

Never truly understanding
A missed expression of tone
An aggressive, defensive response
The tower of Babel crumbling
And the hundreds of tongues creating division
Will you be here to see the unifying
As we all understand each other
As though by magic
The tongues of heaven
Gibberish or intelligible
Either way, now you know the word for ball
Soon colours and numbers
These will create relationships
And on them your first verbal steps
And on them we build nations
And end them

Anxiety

There are stories that were once told around camp fires
But now are relayed by beauty experts on youtube
The lost ones, but only the ones we find
In ways we wish we didn't
And those who are responsible
Their names clumped around the 70s
In the years where our mothers were young
And learning about the world
Learning that it is not a kind place
And it is unsafe for young women
And then upon becoming mothers
When they thought perhaps their demographic was protection
Wrapped around them like a blanket
The locus of their safety trails away
Into the lively limbs of their offspring
When they trail away too far
And the umbilical aches force breath into the lungs
And call them home
For they were mothers in the 90s
When those who took the young became known

Another light shone into a hidden corner of a
cupboard
Overflowing with filth and insects and mould
There are those that are found
And they carry with them the weight of
experience
Far too young
Or not young at all
And the nightmares begin about their children
And they claw to them terrified
For a moment, themselves the child
Do not leave me
I will be broken and lost
Be the comfort
A twisted reversal
The pain of those acts
Done to strangers by strangers
Causing rupture and disfunction in homes a
world away

Being Needed

They talk in hushed tones about the before times
That long forgotten other
It seemed like a different place not just a
different time
When they were in charge of their own
schedules
And they did what they wished
Oh the freedom!
But I cannot relate to this impulse
There was no freedom for me
Just people who needed
Ones who were not really my children
But required mothering just the same
No freedom in this
Only requirement
Justify my existence by helping those around
A mantra that was pre verbal
An inner drive never even needing to be
expressed
There is more freedom in us
Freedom from them
Yes you have needs
And I have them too
But your presence defends me
Sword and shield

Eyes aflame
From them and their grabbing hands
Because others can relate
To being needed by a child
Not so much to being needed by adults
Even less so those who are in an equal
relationship
Even less so those who should be caring for you

Identity

To lose oneself
To feel those glistening particles flitter away
Would be a joy
You have to know yourself to lose yourself
And if you do not know yourself there is nothing
to lose
Is that less painful
Than the echoing empty?
Reflecting on the self seems masturbatory
Experimenting with roles irresponsible
Gaining insight from others codependent
Which way does the path go then?
If there is no freedom to experiment
There is no freedom to know
To really know
To lock in the spine and stand tall
Instead there is the shriveling, sniffling
Curled into nothingness
Even the fingers are curled
And the nails bite into the flesh
Take up as little space as possible
For what role is there for one without a self
Is there a reflection even in the mirror anymore?
Can I build up the pillars like brickwork?
Take one solid thing

And pile it upon the other
Until the sphinx is apparent
The architect pleased
But who is the architect?
Is it you, Father?
Were there plans all along that I was unaware
of?
Or are you just there to pick up the pieces of
whatever I have
Take a barbeque, build it poorly and call it art
Take something useless and call it ornament
Do I wish to be useful or ornamental?
The pictures tell me that I need to be both
To earn my place
To make up for my disgrace
To appease merciless god of industry
To force upon myself clarity
And what will that clarity bring?
But a sense that this was not worth the while
That nothing is.
For identity is only one component of an ever
changing presence
And what is fixed then is my daughterhood
I am yours, so the song goes.
And you are mine.

Becoming and Choices

Identity is such a complex concept
Each category opens ten others
And each of those ten others
Until they become smaller and smaller
Like a concertina file
Open more and more information
Create more and more distinction
Until you can find the specifics
Those unique details
To think yourself unique is narcissistic
To think everyone like you is narcissistic
These identities
Like tarot cards
Shuffle upon the awakening
A whole new self
Presented or decided?
Copy paste shift save
The earth mother appeals
Freedom and unrestricted emotion
Dance in the storm, feeling the wind
Sage and banish the demons
Never wash

But be watched and judged
Not as appealing
Be threatened with ones taken
The home mother appeals too
Cook more than you need
Wrap in love like a blanket
But be formidable to keep the order
Love and fear together
But a loss of self is apparent
Be judged as lacking your muchness
You could be so much more
But there is no time
And so what does one do with this?
Who can one decide to be other than something
incorrect
And who is deciding this anyway?

The Water Drop

The clouds close and the sky darkens and the
storm rolls in
The small water droplet forms from
condensation
It falls
Into a tree's hugging leaves
Down into the soil
Making its way through the layers
Visiting the history of nature
Past a skeleton or two
Rubbish and refuse an unwelcome pit stop
And into the underground system
Joining its brothers and sisters
Into a rushing carnival
Thousands of its kin
Forming the lifesource
It feels peace for a moment
Then, suddenly a new train arrives
It is taken and sucked through pipes
Open into sweet relief as it tumbles down
Into a cold hard glass
The family is fewer now
They are lifted, an opposite sensation to falling
But not unpleasant
Swallowed down into a pool of acid

There small fronds pick them up, one by one
Absorb them across membranes into more rivers
These are of the human kind
A deep beating thumps them around
It is like a rollercoaster
They are blushed and changed
Carrying things here, there and everywhere
A rat race and city of industry inside a body
Then, selected and pushed towards another
A tiny lifeform, much smaller than their host
They become its cushion
The beating is faster and the rollercoaster still
But still exhilarating
Then, great shock, the smaller lifeform is born
There is pressure and the water finds itself
sprayed across cold tiles
There is new life and the droplet's siblings are
pouring down a face
This droplet, though, is headed for the drain
It swings down, it knows how to do all of this
Through a treatment where it is molded and
shaped and cleaned
Until released into the ocean
Where it can rejoin its friends
Their gratitude is salty and they lay in wait
For a warm sun
For the journey to start again

The Shape of the Heart

What is the shape of your heart?
What events internal and external
Of the before and the after
Have altered its biology
And morphed it into something new and foreign
There is so much responsibility
In those first few years
While you are still forming
Your mind and personality being knitted
together
Inside a body that is still learning how to show
itself to the world
It is a more pressured knitting than that of the
womb
When I was ignorant
And did as I was told
Now every decision is in the micro
And the impacts pound through the generations
So what is the shape of your heart?
Is there a cartoon redness
Of something underdeveloped and mass
produced

Are you a number only?
Or is there a toxic heart in there
All metal and wheels and pumping sludge
Producing noxious gas and waste
As it chunders through industry
Or perhaps there is one barely held together
With stiches and gaffer tape
The marks of what I have done
Of what others have done
Forever bleeding slowly
Unable to complete more than a hop a long beat
I wish so desperately to know
And I wont until the die is cast
And I must be content with this

The Carnival

There is a boy
A very broken boy
And he spreads his brokenness around like
confetti
And he is only four years old
And I see you getting a face full
And trying to dust yourself off
But this is the kind that clings
And it does seem so very fun, of course
Because who wouldn't want to be covered in
colours
In a persistent glitter
These are things associated with the good times
Weddings and birthdays and bar mitzvahs
Things to celebrate
So why would you not drink of it
wholeheartedly
So it is with smiles and laughs and heightened
energy
But the energy becomes manic
And out of control
I can see your fear as your emotions run faster
away than even you can catch
A careening train

A maddened laugh before it its off the side of a
mountain
Blain the train in his madness
The confetti has taken on a horror funhouse
sheen
There are laughing clowns
But they are laughing at you
And they are ten feet high
And there is noise everywhere
And hands are reaching
And things are exploding out of canons
And elephants are running wild
And everything is just so loud, loud, loud
In this terrifying circus that only started with a
little confetti
You long so desperately to return to the safety of
the womb
Where nothing was exciting
But also nothing was unexpected
And how I long to clutch you there
And keep everything safe and calm and
considered
But how could I possibly deny you this?
A child I had so long thought of destined for
loneliness
How could I deny you connection and base
friendship?
So we will weather this broken little boy
And line up again for the circus

Because the confetti really is so exciting

Home

As carefully as we take care of our bodies
Plying them with vitamins
Sleeping the right way
Exercising if we can
Sending soothing feelings
Caressing the belly
So carefully do we wish to take care of your
homes
The place you will run to when everything
seems lost
The warm neutral zero
The place to be safe to explore
To grow and change
To love and be loved
And there is such a loss in not being able to
provide this
A place that will one day be a hall of memories
And a place that shifts and changes for you now
There are rules to be followed
And whispered neurosis
That needs must endure
Because who could possibly ever think that the
rich should be the ones who pay when things go
wrong. Who could possibly ever think that the
ones making their wealth and luxury off the

backs of things that are necessary could ever
possibly be unacceptable. Lets mark up the price
of food and medications, all in the name of GDP
while we are at it, meanwhile the poor suffer and
go on living, hoping desperately for a reprieve
that will never come and the shame builds
because we have been sold a lie that those who
have are the ones who worked hard to earn it.
And that means it can be any of us. Because we
all try hard, right? Never mind birthed
privileged, never mind moral conduct. Forget all
of this, because being poor is a character flaw,
and the man Jesus the worst of all sinners.
But
I will shield you from this
We must be careful, but I will fix the destruction
I will patch it back together again
You will not be blamed
For how could anyone possibly blame a child
Who is just trying to be a child
For existing in a world
That doesn't want the inconvenience of children

The Things I Do Not Know

Mother knows best
But this mother knows nothing
Honestly, not a thing
How could I possibly have the slightest idea
About what to expect
We live in unprecedented times, you know
But all times are unprecedented
All children, unprecedented
All lives, unprecedented
For that is what makes them beautiful
I saw once that crows are intelligent
That they are in their version of the stone age
They are using tools superior to our ancestors
And they keep wild dogs as pets and bond with
them
Good for them
We will never see the civilisations they will
build
Our descendants will diminish under the toil of
erasing
A debt accrued by their ancestors
Far too large to ever get out from under

For our whole society runs on debt
Why wouldn't our whole species
Pillaging through time
Erasure eminent
So no, dear child
I do not know
And I can see for a flicker
That this disturbs you
That you had assumed that mothers know all
Is that not comforting?
Not really
If they try to know all and fall short
That is much more disconcerting
Like an icicle drop running down your spine
Rules followed for so long they began to be
common sense
And then forced to be reworked
Relearned
And the accompanying resentment
Ignored
Thrown out with the baby
Sloshing onto the grass

To See Ahead

Just one more
It will always be just one more
The overwhelming desire to clutch to me
Those who I want to heal and bless
But I do not think this is wrong
Perhaps this is the path
It is not everyone's
But many walking on a single road make for a
traffic jam
I prefer the wind in theory
The road where you can't see a minute ahead of
you
To run at break neck speed
But today I am not enjoying the unknown as
much
Today I would like a plan
Even a sign
If at all possible
That this life that I imagine
Is something that can possibly happen
I want the six
I want the congregation
I want the place of our own
And that longing is hitting so close to my heart
That today it hurts

With that subtle aroma of potential
disappointment
To pray, to hope
That is all that is left
And wait
To see what is lying ahead
Just more than a minute ahead

The End

There is such a blessing in the stillness
A moment to reflect
A moment to oneself
A moment to miss you
To write words about our journey together
To write the poetry that has helped the process
And to see all things as beautiful
I once thought that finding beauty was about
finding beauty
It is not.
It is about seeing with a different lens
A lens of stillness
A message told a thousand times
But I learn wisdom slowly
And only through experience, it seems
And so I finish this season
Of writing out my thoughts in my words
And it doesn't feel like an end, but a beginning
The cliché of all clichés
An appropriate way to end